How to Build a Profitable Speaking Business

Rave Reviews

"Bret Has Made a Profound Impact at My Events"

"In the business development industry, none of us can afford to make the mistake of sharing our stages with well-known "experts" who dazzle but don't deliver. Our audiences need substance, integrity, and how-to information. Anything less is unfair to them and a stain on our reputation. I've learned to be meticulously careful about who gets on my stage and that's why I always say "yes" to Bret Ridgway.

Bret has made a profound impact at my events. His knowledge of the industry is strong, his ethics are unwavering, and my audiences always appreciate his willingness to go the extra mile to provide practical advice when he leaves the stage. I enthusiastically recommend Bret for any event promoters who demand only the best for the people they serve."

Wendy Lipton-Dibner, President & CEO
Professional Impact, Inc.

"Bret is an Information Marketer's Best Friend"

"Bret Ridgway is an info marketer's best friend. Bret is great because he really likes and understands the business. He's IN the business. He's a speaker, author and an info publisher himself. And, he really cares about you. He really gets to know what you're doing and looks for ways to give you what you want, what you've asked for, and also to improve upon the process. He will help you take what you're doing to the next level."

David Garfinkel, Author
Breakthrough Copywriting

"Always a Big Hit with Our Authors"

"At Morgan James Publishing, we do a live Red-Carpet Event for our new authors and have brought Bret in to share his expertise with them. Bret's practical, no-nonsense tips about the publishing industry are always a big hit with our authors!"

David L. Hancock
Founder, Morgan James Publishing

"Knew How to Speak Right to My Audience"

"Bret was an excellent guest on the podcast and has a wealth of knowledge to share ranging from events and speaking to fulfilling orders to books to good business relationships. He knew how to speak right to my audience on how they can grow their business as authors and added so much great value as well. Thank you, Bret for coming on!"

Katelyn Silva
WeWriteBooks.com

"People Loved Your Talk!"

"I was so pleased to have you as part of our Awakening Author Book Writing Telesummit and am deeply appreciative of the authentic and insightful contributions you brought to the circle. People loved your talk about the speaking industry!"

Susan Crossman, Founder
Awakening Author Book Writing Telesummit

"Great Tool For a Beginning Speaker"

"*How to Build a Profitable Speaking Business* is terrific and is a great tool for a beginning speaker or even a blogger or course developer. It's obvious you know your business!"

Helen Schram Cole
TheJeanCollective.ca

"The 21 Tips Shared in How to Build a Profitable Speaking Business are Pure Gold"

"Having known Bret for nearly 30 years now, I can assure you that Bret has an inside look into the speaking business. He's had a vantage point that many in this industry haven't seen. The informational 21 tips shared in *How to Build a Profitable Speaking Business* are pure gold and spot on info culled from his astute observations being in the speaking industry and a published author himself."

Frank Deardurff
ThatOneWebGuy.com

"Anybody Aspiring to Make a Success as a Speaker Needs to Read How to Build a Profitable Speaking Business"

"Anybody aspiring to make a success as a speaker absolutely needs to read *How to Build a Profitable Speaking Business*. It's highly readable, highly practical, and it will save you from wasting both time and money. This is solid gold: 21 priceless nuggets from every aspect of the speaking business."

Dr. Margaret Winters
CreateWholeBodyHealth.com

"Valuable Gift to Anyone Who Values His Time"

"Bret is transferring a legacy thru his valuable lines from his real time encounters. *How to Build a Profitable Speaking Business* is taking me up to persona of a price worthy person as a speaker. It's a valuable gift to anyone who values his time in his life."

V.K.Anil Kumar
AnilsCareerGuidance.com

"Bret Ridgway Ignites That Passion to be Heard with His No-Nonsense Approach"

"Wondering how to share a message that you feel strongly about is different from the need to share your message. Bret Ridgway ignites that passion to be heard with his no-nonsense approach to making your ideas a reality.

He makes speaking to a receptive audience an easy opportunity to ignite a movement while building your business. His tips and insights provide you with background and forethought for a successful presentation. My favorite tip is #1 The Back Pocket Speech, because we should all be ready to share our message at a moment's notice, with ease and calm."

Michelle Greenwell
DanceDebut.com
Linktr.ee/dancedebut

"Practical Advice and Knowledge"

"As a new speaker it was so nice to receive no-nonsense tips from Bret. Now having more tools for building this business, I feel confident to take that next step and use these tools to begin the journey towards the speaking business. Thank you, Bret, for your honesty, practical advice and knowledge".

Carlamay Sheremata

"Definitely a Must-Read for All Speakers"

"*How to Build a Profitable Speaking Business* about speaking is definitely a must-read for all speakers new and seasoned! I've been speaking for over 20 years and got some great reminders from reading *How to Build a Profitable Speaking Business*. In fact, I can't wait to buy it and give it to all my clients so they have a guide to go by when they're trying to profit more from speaking in their businesses too.

I think there are more than 21 tips here. It's more like five or six tips inside each main topic. I especially like the advice around being open to and recognizing all opportunities around you. Also, looking at your metrics because most speakers don't pay attention and speak blindly all over the place, without focus on to whom, how many, etc. and then don't make money. Great job at capturing all the possible things speakers need to know about all types of different speaking opportunities!"

Katrina Sawa

The Jumpstart Your Biz Coach, Publisher and Best-selling Author with JumpstartYourBizNow.com, JumpstartPublishing.net and Founder of the International Speaker Network at iSpeakerNetwork.com

"Walks You Through the Phases Required to Develop a Successful Speaking Career"

"I just finished Bret Ridgway's book, *How to Build a Profitable Speaking Business*. I am not a speaker, however, after finishing *How to Build a Profitable Speaking Business* I believe I could be! *How to Build a Profitable Speaking Business* literally walks you through the phases required to develop a successful speaking career in clear, concise terms, including how to sell your product from the stage, as well as the pitfalls to avoid. Bret has just produced a brilliant road map to a successful speaking career."

Share Munoz, Producer
ViviaDigitalFilms.com

"Full of Golden Nuggets"

"Thanks for the excellent book, Bret! *How to Build a Profitable Speaking Business* has given me many insights on how I can take my professional speaking business to the next level. *How to Build a Profitable Speaking Business* is full of golden nuggets, without any fluff. Each of the 21 tips can help people at all levels wanting to increase their speaking opportunities and uncover many secret strategies that could 10X the growth of your profitable speaking business."

Akshay Ash Goel
GrowthXSchool.com

"Clear, Concise and Right on Point"

"Bret Ridgway's *How to Build a Profitable Speaking Business* is exactly what I need. It's clear, concise and absolutely right on point. The techniques are simple to do, so there's no excuse. Read it, do it, find bookings and get paid."

Ronnie Tsunami
CEO and Founder of Rock You Academy

"Bret Reveals the Truth"

"Bret brings the value. His professionalism and expertise are well known in the speaking industry. I was grateful to get help from Bret back in 2006 when I put together my credit repair course and set out to sell from the stage and help people benefit from what I'd learned in the mortgage business. What I didn't know was vast—but with Bret's knowledge and direction I was able to successfully sell from the stage.

Until you've been in the business for years, you don't learn the things you really need to know...so Bret put them all in *How to Build a Profitable Speaking Business* for you. Dealing with event promoters, keeping control of your presentation and money—Bret reveals the truth about how the speaking business operates and saves you from the heartache of learning the hard way. *How to Build a Profitable Speaking Business* is very complete—if you haven't started your speaking career yet (or even if you have) this is the book that will launch your career with the exact information you need to be successful."

Lucy Brenton
www.LucyBrenton.com

How To Build A
PROFITABLE
Speaking Business

21 Tips for Taking Your
Speaking Business
To the NEXT Level

BRET RIDGWAY

NEW YORK

LONDON • NASHVILLE • MELBOURNE • VANCOUVER

How to Build a Profitable Speaking Business

21 Tips for Taking Your Speaking Business to the Next Level

Published in New York, New York, by Morgan James Publishing. Morgan James is a trademark of Morgan James, LLC. www.MorganJamesPublishing.com

Proudly distributed by Publishers Group West®

A FREE ebook edition is available for you or a friend with the purchase of this print book.

CLEARLY SIGN YOUR NAME ABOVE

Instructions to claim your free ebook edition:
1. Visit MorganJamesBOGO.com
2. Sign your name CLEARLY in the space above
3. Complete the form and submit a photo of this entire page
4. You or your friend can download the ebook to your preferred device

ISBN 9781636981253 paperback
ISBN 9781636981260 ebook
Library of Congress Control Number:
2023930413

Cover Design by:
Frank Deardurff
iMakeBookCovers.com

Interior Design by:
Chris Treccani
www.3dogcreative.net

Morgan James is a proud partner of Habitat for Humanity Peninsula and Greater Williamsburg. Partners in building since 2006.

Get involved today! Visit: www.morgan-james-publishing.com/giving-back

Table of Contents

Foreword

Wendy Lipton-Dibner, MA
President and CEO, Professional Impact, Inc.

I had just stepped off the stage when event coordinator Audrey Hagen slid her arm through mine and yelled into my ear, *"Let's get you to the back of the room. There's a big crowd waiting for you!"*

As the tech removed my mic, Audrey grabbed my bag and escorted me out from behind the curtain where hundreds of people were still on their feet, whooping and applauding.

While Audrey shepherded me through the crowd, I locked eyes with men and women whose dreams had led them to this space. I could actually feel their hearts pounding with excitement.

When we finally arrived at the back of the ballroom, I saw why Audrey had been so anxious to get me there. Three long lines had formed in record time, filled with people of all ages.

Everyone stood patiently, happily chatting with new friends as they waited to hand in the three-part form that would assure their seat at my upcoming live event.

As Audrey's team processed the forms, I stood to the side speaking with each person, answering their questions, and sharing hugs.

This continued through lunch and when the audience returned to take their seats, we moved into the hallway out of respect for the next speaker. Moving the table didn't change a thing. They just kept coming—all afternoon and throughout the two days that followed.

On day two of the event, Audrey walked me to one of the sponsored booths to introduce me to a man who would become a trusted vendor for (and sponsor of) my business and a treasured friend. More than a decade later, Bret and I are still connected—now here together with you.

At the end of the weekend, Audrey handed me copies of the forms that had been turned in. I was profoundly honored (and frankly shocked) by the result: 78% of attendees had registered to attend my live event!

The event promoter gave me a big hug and invited me to come back for his next event. As I walked away, I overheard him telling another speaker he'd *"discovered"* me and that I had become, *"an overnight success."*

I couldn't help but smile. I'd been a professional speaker for over three decades.

I'd spoken at well over 1,000 events—professional conferences in every industry from healthcare to haircare;

private corporate and non-profit events; and in-house trainings around the globe.

I'd had the privilege of speaking in massive arenas and intimate venues, the honor of receiving countless standing ovations, and the joy of meeting tens of thousands of people along the way.

And yes, I'd been well-compensated for my speaking, receiving five- and six-figure checks and invitations for many other opportunities after each speech.

My bestselling books had been sponsored by major corporations, and one of my books had become required reading at medical and dental colleges.

Most importantly, the walls of my office were filled with thank-you notes from conference attendees, coaching clients, and readers.

Yes, I was a thirty-year, overnight success.

The thing is, over all that time, not one promoter had asked me to sell my products or services at their events. In fact, it was expressly forbidden in every speaking contract I signed.

Granted, I had long ago learned how to plant ethical seeds that would lead professional audiences to purchase my books or hire me as an in-house trainer or consultant, but not once had I overtly sold anything on a stage.

In fact, this was the first time I'd been invited to speak at an event where the promoter *expected* me to sell on the stage *and* give him a percentage of my sales.

I had entered an entirely different world where "success" was measured by transactions, and I wasn't sure I liked it.

You see over my entire career I had never focused on what I would *get* from speaking. It was always about what I would *give*.

- I'd never had a dream to be a multi-million-dollar speaker (although I was).
- I'd never had a vision that I would travel the world as speaker (although I did).
- And never in my wildest imagination did I think I'd be walking through airports where people stopped me to sign their copy of one of my books (although that happened a lot).

The simple truth is I've always had only one business goal: to make a measurable impact in people's lives so *they* in turn would go on to make an impact on every life they touched.

To this day, I tell my audiences the most important truth of business success is:

When you *Focus On Impact*® the money will come.

I've proven that time and again. Yet while focusing on impact is the foundation of success, it's not *all* you need to do to be successful.

You can't make your impact as a speaker if you don't get on stages, podcasts, webinars, etc.

You can't expand your impact beyond speaking unless you create products and services people will buy and use and love and then tell all their friends to buy and use and love.

You can't live the lifestyle you want to live until you have enough money to hire people to do all the things that need to be done so you're free to get the most out of every day.

The simple truth is:

If you want your impact to be profoundly felt, you need to build a business that is strategically and operationally designed to enable you to make the impact you were born to bring the world.

This isn't hard to do, but it can take forever if you try to do it on your own. Frankly, life is far too short for that nonsense.

That's why I'm excited Bret has written this book.

Bret has taken decades of on-the-ground experience and culled it down into the critical things we need to do to thrive as speakers.

He has simplified profitability for speakers into twenty-one tips—each of which is gold.

You can read this book in less than an hour, but when you're done the secret is to *go back and read it again—slowly.* Look carefully at each tip and decide how it fits for your unique impact!

This book is a golden checklist for making money as a speaker—an actual **treasure trove of tips you can use to get paid for your impact**.

Of course, at some point you'll want to go deeper with step-by-step, how-to information, and Bret has listed some great resources (including his own courses) that you can use to get there.

The key is: don't waste time and money trying to figure this out on your own.

Because somewhere out there is a community of people who are waiting for your impact to appear. Please don't make them wait.

Follow Bret's tips and get your impact out to the people who need you.

Do it now, because life is far too short to settle for less than you truly want—in your business or your life.

To your impact!

Wendy Lipton-Dibner

Introduction

The speaking industry is a fascinating one, with thousands upon thousands of men and women, young and old, of all nationalities and ethnicities calling themselves a speaker. If you are reading this then you either consider yourself to be, or wish to be, one of that unique breed we call a speaker.

We've all heard the old line that the number one fear of most people is public speaking. Even more than death. If you have that fear, any internet search will uncover a wealth of resources aimed at helping people overcome the fear of public speaking. If you're one of those that needs that confidence boost, then by all means you should pursue those resources.

We also see a wealth of resources online focused on getting speaking gigs. Whether you're a keynote (fee) speaker or a back-of-the-room seller (free) speaker, or both, the overall success of your speaking business will largely depend upon the number of gigs you are able to land. Doesn't matter whether it's a live event, a virtual summit or a podcast. Got to get those gigs!

Whether it's through a speaker bureau, through your own relationship marketing efforts, through pay-per-click advertising, through social media or any other channel, getting that next speaking engagement is critical to both your short- and long-term success. You certainly do need to master the art and science of landing speaking engagements.

While continual improvement of your speaking skills and getting gigs are both critical elements of achieving success as a speaker, they are just two of the many aspects of building a successful speaking business. This book will focus not just on those, but on all the aspects of building a profitable speaking business. It's not simply about trading time for dollars—it's about generating a profit that will help you lead the life you want to lead, support the causes you want to support and truly have a positive impact on the world.

In my twenty-five plus years in the speaking industry I've been a conference attendee, I've been a speaker, I've managed the back-of-the-room sales table at nearly 150 separate events and I've founded a company that handled the production and fulfillment of the products for many of the top names in the speaking world. Eventually I shared the stage with some of those top names.

My unique behind-the-scenes perspective from the back-of-the-room and as the fulfillment partner for the top dogs has enabled me to see what works and what doesn't work in the speaking world. I've seen great successes and I've witnessed miserable failures of speakers.

I've had event promoters crying on my shoulder because they didn't understand how to work with hotels properly. I've seen speakers sell $375,000 of product at an event and then need to refund every penny. I've witnessed scheduled speakers carted off in an ambulance and watched the panicked promoter try to figure out what to do.

Yes, this book is about helping you to build a PROFITABLE speaking business. But it's also about helping you to avoid some of the stupid things I've seen speakers do. And avoiding those mistakes will definitely lead to a more profitable and successful speaking business.

To your success!

Bret Ridgway

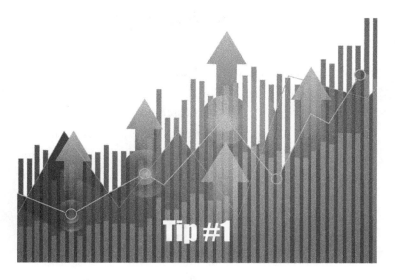

Tip #1

The Back Pocket Speech

As I watched my friend and colleague being loaded onto a gurney and placed in the waiting ambulance, I glanced over at the event promoter. What I saw in his eyes literally bordered on a state of panic. Sure, he was concerned about my friend, but he was also concerned about his event.

You see, the person being loaded into that ambulance was scheduled to be the very next speaker on the agenda. I could see the wheels turning in the promoter's brain as he struggled to come up with a solution. "What am I going to do? How am I going to fill up his ninety-minute slot? How do I keep the flow of my event moving forward in

1

a positive manner? How do I deliver on the promises I've made to my attendees?"

We've probably all witnessed it at some time or another—an unexpected disruption to an event that can create havoc for the event promoter. Maybe it's a sudden medical emergency that means the scheduled speaker can't take the stage. Or maybe it's the no show speaker who leaves a gaping time slot without warning.

While either situation is unfortunate, as a speaker at an event where something like this occurs, you need to recognize it for the opportunity it is and to be prepared to act fast.

That event promoter is looking for a solution to his problem. He doesn't want to have to tap dance for those ninety minutes (or however long a speaking slot is at that conference) to fill the hole in his agenda. Here's a chance for you to come to their rescue and help him keep the event moving forward in a positive manner.

How? By having what I call the "back pocket" speech. The back pocket speech is a second talk you are prepared to deliver at a moment's notice to the audience. Of course, it should be related to the primary focus of the event. Ideally, I also think it should be a content-only presentation.

You can provide the event promoter a solution to his problem by offering to take that now open speaking slot and deliver some great content to his attendees. How does it benefit you?

1. You'll have the gratitude of the event promoter. When they plan future events, you'll be top of mind for their speaker list.
2. You'll have more face time with the attendees. Handled properly, this additional time with the audience should help you to build even better rapport and, if you're selling a product or service at the back of the room after your other presentation, increase those back of the room sales.
3. It gives you another opportunity to deliver that secondary presentation and get even more comfortable with it should you need to deliver it at another conference.

Building a Profitable Speaking Business is About Being Prepared to Seize Opportunities When They Present Themselves

---

Building a profitable speaking business is about being prepared to seize those opportunities when they present themselves. Your back pocket speech should be a standard part of your speaker's toolkit. Maybe you'll never need it. But don't be the one kicking yourself when that opportunity comes up and you aren't prepared to take advantage of it because you don't have a back pocket speech prepared.

**Scan the QR Code to Get on
The Notification List for the Next
"From Novice Speaker to Stage Ready Pro"
Masterclass
or
Visit BretRidgway.com and click on
the Consulting Tab**

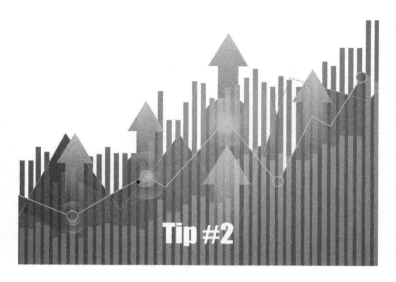

Tip #2

Relationship Management

helped develop a fulfillment company that was built entirely from meeting people at live events and the subsequent word-of-mouth advertising. Pay-per-click advertising was in its infancy and no other paid advertising was done to build what would become a multi-million-dollar company.

Relationships Are Your Single Most Important Business Asset

Relationships are, without a doubt, your single most important business asset. Not your website, your office, your logo or anything else. It is those people you have developed a relationship with who will be your biggest supporters and who, in turn, you should be the biggest supporters of.

To believe you can sit behind your computer all day and build a profitable speaking business is, in my opinion, foolhardy. You've got to get out there and meet people and get to know people and have them get to know you. Virtual meetings can be great and have become an important part of business today. But there is no substitute for meeting a person face to face and sharing a drink or a meal with them.

You must approach it with a "What can I do for you attitude" as opposed to always looking at what they can do for you. And you must sincerely mean it.

A few years ago, a book I'd co-written titled *Mistakes Authors Make* became an Amazon #1 Bestseller solely because of the relationships I'd established in the speaking industry over the previous fifteen years. When help was needed to promote a launch date for the book, my friends and colleagues were happy to help because of the relationship I had with them.

I'm also a big believer in the power of the handwritten thank you note. Services such as Send Out Cards are great, but they're just not the same as receiving a personally written note (in blue ink). Simply have your logo printed on the front of some blank note cards. Be sure to include your contact information on the back of the card. After all, it is a marketing piece.

Almost every person I meet at an event will receive a note from me. Every new client that comes on board will receive a note. And they express their gratitude almost 100% of the time. It's remembered.

So, as a speaker, who should you think about building relationships with? Here are a few:

- Event Promoters—Who's going to put you on the platforms? That's right, the event promoters. So, get to know as many of them as you possibly can.
- Fellow Speakers—Some of your best referral partners for speaking engagements can be other speakers. When a promoter is looking for one more speaker, they'll often ask their existing speakers who they might recommend. Or, if a speaker isn't available for a specific engagement themselves, maybe they'll suggest the promoter contact you.
- Audio & Video Crew—Maybe you want to host your own events in the future. Wouldn't it be better to know people in the industry who can provide audio and video at your event?
- Hotel Contacts—Again, maybe you want to do your own events in the future. Having already built a rapport with a catering manager or the person in charge of room setup can serve you well.

On another note, remember that your presentation begins as soon as you set foot on site. If you're rude to a hotel bellman or the event promoter, or if a fellow speaker or attendee notices your bad behavior, you'll create a hurdle you must overcome to establish a positive relationship with that person.

RELATIONSHIPS. ARE. CRITICAL.

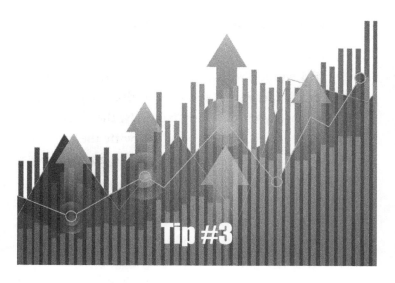

Nurturing Your Flock

So many people (myself included) have built up fairly large lists and then not followed up regularly enough with the people on that list. You need to maintain regular communication with your followers and always continue to build that know, like and trust factor.

I've seen industry statistics that claim around 30% of people's email addresses change annually. I have no way of knowing how accurate that number is, but if it's anywhere close to that, then it's a pretty significant loss every year. If you haven't kept your name in front of them with regular email communication, they are simply going to forget about you. Then, when their email address changes, they're not engaged enough with you to even think about updating their email address in your system. Bye bye prospect.

If you email your followers regularly, they'll get a feel for the "tone" of your conversations with them. It will become a part of your brand and you've got to protect your brand very carefully.

Several years ago, I was having lunch with a colleague who works in the financial services industry. He was telling me about a list he had built up to around 55,000 people. A pretty significant following. He had been communicating with them regularly and they had a certain expectation about what they were going to get from him when he emailed.

Then he decided to enlist the help of an internet "guru" to help him with an email campaign. A message went out that was so polar opposite of what his followers had come to expect from him that it began to happen immediately—Unsubscribe—Unsubscribe—Unsubscribe. When all was said and done, a list that had been 55,000 people was now a list of just 5,000 people. Ouch! You've got to be very cognizant of your brand and be careful how you nurture those that are part of your world. Anyone involved in communication with your followers must know how you've communicated with them in the past.

It's important to remember that all your nurturing doesn't have to be online in the form of email. I have a colleague who has the longest running coaching program in the internet marketing world—nearly twenty years and going strong! And while the crux of his training and coaching is all about online marketing, he still sends his members a physical magazine every month. If we play only in the digital world, it's so easy to get out of sight, out of mind. That offline touch is a regular reminder of the value he is bringing to his clients.

If you have a large group of followers or VIP attendees at your event, then you might want to consider what we call a swag kit. It could include items like t-shirts, coffee mugs, journals, pens, notepads, or any number of other things. You need to recognize those that are paying to be part of your flock so they want to stay.

> It's Important to Nurture Those Who Have Stepped Into Your World So They Want To Remain in Your World

Maintaining regular communication with your flock in some form or other is an essential part of building a profitable speaking business. So, how do your nurturing efforts stack up?

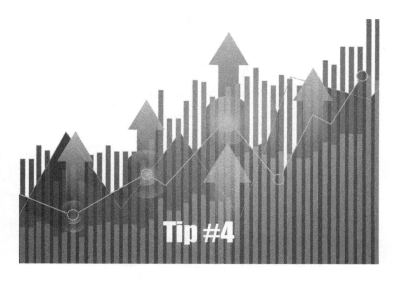

Event Promoters

Event promoters are an interesting breed. If you've been around the block more than once you've probably learned they tend to be overly optimistic about the number of people who will attend their event, whether it's in person or a virtual event.

This is especially true if they are a first-time promoter. They speak in terms of "wishes" rather than realities. I'm not implying they are being intentionally misleading—it is more that they are overly optimistic about the size of the crowd they will actually be able to get into their meeting room when the event happens.

Bear in mind that the number of registrations doesn't mean the number of attendees. A virtual event that offers a free ticket will typically have about a 30% show rate.

As a speaker, it is of paramount importance that you find out as far as possible in advance of an event how many people will be in the room. We talked about metrics already—those numbers you should track from event to event to monitor your own performance.

These same metrics—number of attendees, number of actual buying units, and closing percentages—are all numbers that a professional promoter may be able to provide you from their previous events. They may be able to show you a spreadsheet from their earlier events that break down the sales figures by speaker (anonymously, of course).

You know you are dealing with a professional promoter when they can provide this data for you easily. If they are unable to, chances are you may be dealing with a first-time promoter who does not have any historical data. Or you're dealing with a promoter who is being less than forthcoming with you. If you think that's the case, you should enter that relationship with your eyes wide open.

An event promoter should always be willing to share with you who else is going to be on their platform. Are all the speaking slots ones that sell to the crowd, or are they interspersing content-only sessions throughout the event?

Promoters should be able to tell you each speaker's topic, the length of each speaking slot, and at what price point the other speakers' offers are going to be.

If the promoter has held previous events, they should be able to provide you the demographics of their audience and what has worked well in regard to price point and type of products or services offered to their crowd. This will be beneficial to you.

Remember, promoters put on events to make money. In an ideal world, most hope to make enough money from advance ticket sales to cover their out-of-pocket costs for putting on the event. That means their split of the back-of-the-room sales is where they really make their profit, and anything they can do to help you succeed on their platform is only of benefit to them. They are in it for the money.

Another key detail to work out with a promoter is your assigned speaking slot. There are certain speakers who are fantastic closers and, if they appear on the platform just before you, might suck all the money out of the room and your closing percentages may drop dramatically.

If you have any sway with the promoter at all, you will want to make sure you are speaking before this person rather than after. As far as the best speaking slots at an event, most speakers I know prefer to be either the second speaker in the morning or the second in the afternoon. They want to be sure there is an adequate break scheduled after the conclusion of their presentation so they have time to answer questions and help at the sales table before another speaker gets on stage and commands their attention.

That said, there are other speakers who love to speak first thing in the morning and make it work very well. And there are those who want to be the event closer and do a great job at it.

When you are first beginning your speaking career, you will probably have very little input on your assigned speaking slot. Be fully prepared to "pay your dues" and accept some early morning slots or other typically non-desired times. It is part of the game.

Vendors are a variable that can also influence your sales at an event. If the promoter is having exhibitors, that will usually have an impact on the back-of-the-room sales, as those vendors may also be pulling money from the crowd. Again, this is something you are probably not going to have any control over, but you do need to recognize the impact it can have on your sales numbers.

By and large, promoters are there to help you. They want to see you succeed because your success puts money in their pocket. Just be sure you understand where they are coming from and that it is their rules you need to follow if you want to play in their sandbox.

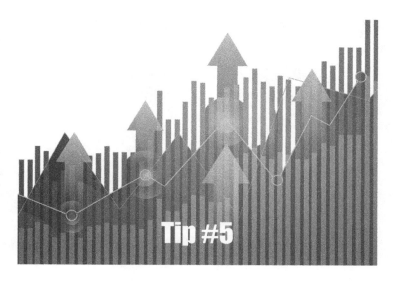

Demographics

Without question, one of the major contributors to the successful delivery of a speech is to have each member of your audience feel as if you are talking directly to them. Your ability to connect at a "heart level" greatly increases the bond you have with your audience and leads to a well-received presentation.

It doesn't matter if your speech is a keynote presentation or a platform selling situation, if you understand the demographics of your audience, you can better tailor your content to connect at a deeper level with the crowd.

So, what do you need to know about the audience before a presentation that might help you do a better job? This list is not all-inclusive, but it is a good starting point:

- Is your audience primarily male or female?
- What is the average age of the audience? Are you talking to teens, baby boomers, senior citizens, etc.
- What is their educational background?
- What type(s) of businesses are represented in the audience?
- Is it a G—PG—PG 13—R—or "F Bomb" type of crowd?
- Have you delivered a presentation to this same audience previously?
- If it is a multiple speaker event, who else is sharing the platform and what will they be talking about?

Much of this information should be available from the event promoter. Large events that have been held many times in the past often have sponsorship packets that contain demographic information about the attendees because they are trying to attract sponsorship money. You can use this information to learn more about the audience.

If you are delivering a keynote presentation, particularly to a single corporate client, you will want to do some research to figure out who the "movers and shakers" are within the audience. A great way to find this information is to simply call the main switchboard of the company for which you will be presenting. Explain you are delivering a keynote for them at their upcoming event and ask the gatekeeper about the key people who will be attending.

You would be amazed at the kind of information you can gather that will enable you to craft your presentation specifically for that company. When you have the ability to acknowledge key people in the audience during the course of your presentation, you really can connect at a much deeper level.

Remember, the more you can address the specific pain point(s) of the group you will be speaking to, the more receptive your audience will be to your presentation. When they feel you are talking directly to them, you come across as much more professional because you have taken the time to truly understand their needs and to deliver information that will benefit them.

These "pain points" are the critical elements you should incorporate into your presentation. More specifically, your solution for those pain points is what will truly ingratiate you with your audience.

Do not hesitate to do some keyword research in advance of an event to try to find out what questions are being asked online related to your topic. The more you can tie in the current things people are seeking solutions for into your presentation, the better you should do.

Now, in a platform selling situation there are some additional pieces of information you will want to gather in advance that could potentially increase your back-of-the-room sales. Ask the event promoter these questions, but do not take the word of the promoter as "gospel."

If you are speaking at an event that has been held before, find out who has spoken at the event previously. Ask the promoter about the price point of each speaker, particularly that of the one who had the most success, plus the subject of their topic.

In general, what price point gets the most action for that promoter's events? If you come in with a $2000 offer and the crowd has only been exposed to $500 price points in the past, you could greatly decrease your chances for success.

Admittedly, sometimes it is difficult to get this information from the promoter. But if you explain you want to do the best job possible for them at the event, they will usually understand and be as forthcoming as possible.

Another great source of information about what worked and did not work at previous events is from those people who provided testimonials for the last event. If you look at the promotional website for the upcoming event you will typically find testimonials from previous attendees. It is pretty easy to find these people online and ask them questions about the event.

Also, once you have been around the speaking circuit for a while, you will have built a trusting relationship with speaking colleagues who are willing to share their experiences with you about working with different promoters.

If you have a contract with an event promoter for an upcoming event (and you always should), then you will want to make sure it doesn't preclude you from adjusting your offer or price point at the event if you see certain things are not working with other speakers. A reasonable promoter will be willing to work with you because they have a vested interest in your success.

Knowing as much about your audience as possible before delivering a presentation seems like a no brainer. You would be surprised at the number of speakers who are unwilling to take the time to get to know their audience in advance so they can finetune their presentation for that audience. Does it take a little bit of work? Of course it does.

You may want to enlist a support person to help with some aspects of your audience marketing research. Whether you do it all yourself or someone helps you, the time invested in getting to know your upcoming audience better can pay massive dividends for you over the long haul.

People definitely buy from those they know, like and trust. Whether it is simply "buying" your message or about buying your product or service, your ability to craft a presentation that is as laser-focused as possible to the needs of your audience can only be done if you really know your audience well. When you do your research, your know, like, and trust factor can grow exponentially.

Your Ability to Craft a Presentation Laser-Focused To Your Audience Can Only Be Done If You Know Your Audience Well

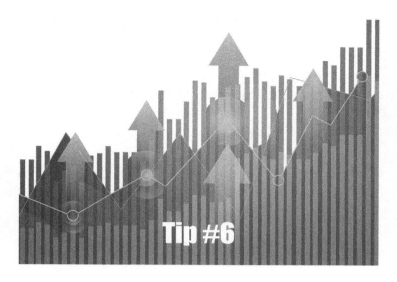

Tip #6

Metrics

When running any business, there's an old expression—"You've got to know your numbers." Yet it is surprising that most business owners have little knowledge of what their key numbers, or metrics, are.

Baseball players have their batting average, investors have their ROI, internet marketers have their click through rate and so on. Each industry has its own set of metrics, and the speaking profession is certainly no different.

What metrics do you need to look at as a speaker? If you make your living by back-of-the-room sales, then there are several key numbers you must know and track about each event. These include:

- Number of attendees
- Number of buying units
- Closing percentage

Number of Attendees

This one is fairly obvious. How many people are in the room at the beginning of your presentation and how many are in the room at the conclusion? Don't try to count them yourself. Enlist the aid of your assistant if you brought one to the event, or get the help of someone else you know and trust to do this for you. It is important to get both the starting and ending counts. Don't ever take the promoter's word on the number of people in the room—double check it.

With a large crowd, you may find it difficult to get an accurate count. If you arrive at the event early, do a count of how many people the room is set up for. This figure may help you get a more accurate estimate if you are forced to go that route.

Number of Buying Units

While similar to the number of attendees, it is not the same thing. A husband and wife attending together are counted as two attendees, but are considered one buying unit. Why? Because both are unlikely to buy the same product at an event.

A few years ago, I attended an event aimed at the home school market. Parents were encouraged to bring their entire families to the event and there were nearly 100 people in attendance. However, when you got down to figuring the number of fathers, mothers, sons and daughters in the audience, you soon realized that 100 people actually represented only about twenty buying units.

Determining the actual number of buying units in a room can be very challenging. In addition to family units, there may be business partners, a business owner and his assistant or even an entire team in the audience. All add to the trickiness of determining the actual number of buying units in the crowd.

You should also factor in things such as the number of other speakers and their assistants. Some may be hanging around after their presentation or coming into the room early to get the lay of the land and size up the crowd prior to their speaking slot. Although other speakers may occasionally buy another speaker's product, you typically wouldn't consider them buying units when figuring your metrics.

Similarly, the event staff itself should not be counted among your buying units or number of attendees. They are there to assist the event promoter and could be doing anything from running microphones, to manning a camera or audio board, to passing out handouts or assisting at the sales table. Many are volunteers, and if one of them happens to buy your product or service, consider it an unexpected bonus.

If possible, see if the event promoter can provide you with a list of attendees prior to the event. Of course, there will always be additions and deletions to an attendee list once the event is underway, but a study of the attendee list in advance can help you determine the number of actual buying units as closely as possible.

Closing Percentage

Why is the number of buying units so critical? Because it is the number on which our third metric—closing percentage—should be based. The closing percentage is the key metric many event promoters will want to know when they are considering putting you on their stage. Do not ever inflate your numbers. If you lie about how well you have sold at other events, you will eventually be found out and your credibility will be forever tarnished. Event promoters do talk and believe me, word will get around.

Once you have determined as best you can the actual number of buying units in the room, then figuring your closing percentage is simply a matter of dividing the number of units of your product or service you sold by the number of buying units in the room.

Here's a couple of simple examples just to be sure you understand.

Example 1:
100 buying units in the room
14 units sold
Closing percentage = 14/100 = 14%

Example 2:
500 buying units in the room
75 units sold
Closing percentage = 75/500 = 15%

If you offer more than one product from the platform, such as a Beginner Package A and an Advanced Package B, consider the sale of either of them as one unit sold, then combine the sales of both to figure your total units sold.

Another factor to consider are livestream numbers. If the event includes a virtual audience, find out from the promoter how many people were logged in during your presentation, along with any sales that came from this audience. Be sure to factor this number into your total when assessing your performance at an event.

Testing and Tracking

It is important to track your performance from event to event. Equally important to tracking is the concept of testing. There are several variables a professional speaker might track to see how they impact his or her personal results.

You will have to determine which variables you want to test to see the effect on your results. It is important to test just one variable at a time. Otherwise, how will you know which variable impacted your results? And only over multiple tests will you be able to draw any meaningful conclusions.

There are always variables which you may not be able to control that can impact your results. Do the best you can with those things you can control.

What are some of the factors that speakers have been known to track and test? Here are just a few:

- For a man, suit with tie vs. suit without a tie
- For a woman, business suit vs. brightly colored dress
- Title of your presentation
- Your offer
- Inclusion or exclusion of different bonuses
- Temperature of room
- How certain key parts of your presentation are worded
- PowerPoint vs. no PowerPoint
- Product to be delivered at the event vs. shipped later
- Physical vs. digital product
- Speaking time slot
- Speaker you followed or preceded
- Demographics of audience
- Male vs. female buyers of your offer

This is certainly only a partial list. There are many other variables one could seriously track and test.

The Professional Speaker Is Meticulous About Testing and Tracking

---

But the professional speaker is meticulous about tracking and testing as many things as they can over time to determine which factors provide him or her with the maximum probability for success.

If you are going to be that professional speaker, be sure you know your metrics, and to track and test those things that could influence your results. It will mean more money in your pocket and help provide you with the dream speaking career you envisioned for yourself.

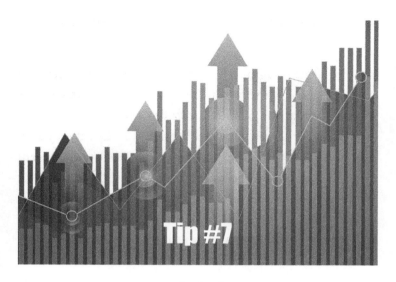

Tip #7

Scalability

L ast time I checked, there are still twenty-four hours in a day and 365 days in a year. That means, as a speaker, you have a very limited number of hours in a day and days in the year you can speak live.

Whether you're a high dollar keynote speaker or the person who speaks for free but generates your revenue by selling in the back of the room, there are some practical limitations to how much you can earn as a speaker unless you can figure out how to scale your business without it all being done by you.

Scalability is critical to the growth of any business. Whether you're running a donut shop, a fulfillment company or a speaking business, there will be factors that can constrain your growth. As a speaker, I don't think there's any doubt that the biggest constraint is time.

Think about it. If you're a keynote speaker, then you're probably going into a corporation gathering or other event for one day. In most cases you're going to have a day of travel in front of the speaking engagement and probably a day of travel on the back side. That means, in reality, you can probably only do a maximum of fifty-two keynotes per year. Could be a few more or a few less depending on how things fall, but you get the idea. There is a definite time constraint.

If you're a back of the room seller, then most events are three days long. With a day of travel on either end you're tying up five calendar days per engagement. So, maybe you can only do thirty-five to forty events per year. Once again, a massive time constraint.

To combat this unyielding time constraint, you must figure out answers to the scalability problem. Here's just a few ideas for you to consider:

#1 Prerecorded Presentations

If you're doing live speaking engagements in order to sell your products or services at the back of the room, then there's no reason you can't record your presentation and put it online as a prerecorded webinar that people can watch 24/7. There are many webinar platforms on the market that can either serve up your presentation on demand or at prescheduled times.

#2 Recurring Revenue

Multiple speakers have told me that their biggest regret is not developing a recurring revenue component to their speaking business earlier. If you're selling at a conference, what can you put together to generate a recurring revenue stream? Maybe it's a coaching program or maybe it's some type of membership site or software as a service.

#1 Regret of Most Speakers is Not Developing A Recurring Revenue Component to Their Speaking Business Sooner

---

The comfort of knowing what revenue you already have scheduled to come in next month is immeasurable. You're not just relying on when you can land that next speaking gig to generate revenue.

#3 The Franchise Model

Is what you teach people something you can teach others to do? Think Fred Pryor, John Maxwell and CareerTrack, for example. Can you systematize what you teach and how you teach it, and have others do it under your umbrella? In essence, we're talking about a franchise or licensing model where others will pay you for the right to use your knowledge and training materials.

#4 Raise Your Rates

Keynote speakers should consider an increase in their rates and every platform seller should consider raising their prices. Generating more revenue for the same amount of work is, in effect, scaling.

By its very nature, the speaking business is a business generally constrained by the time element. Anything you can do as a speaker to leverage your time and efforts to scale your business will lead to a more profitable speaking business.

Tip #8

Getting Gigs

Certainly, the overall profitability of your speaking business will primarily depend on your ability to land speaking engagements. Yes, you need to manage your speaking business effectively and invest money into your business appropriately. But increased sales can cover up a lot of other woes.

The responsibility for generating those increased sales falls directly on you. You may have a team working on your behalf, either internal or external, but don't expect things to magically happen. You must proactively and continuously work to generate new business.

Don't make the mistake of relying on a single source for generating new speaking opportunities. If that particular lead source stops working effectively, then your business could be in serious trouble. Our fulfillment company grew out of relationships built by attending live events. When COVID hit in 2019, live events went away and our primary source of new business went away with them.

So, what are some of the primary ways you can generate additional speaking gigs?

Referrals

Your "easiest" sales will always come from people who are directly referred to you by someone who knows you. That's why continually developing and strengthening relationships with others in the industry is so vitally important. You need to put systems into place that will help generate on-going referrals. Don't just assume they'll happen—you must help make them happen. There are some excellent books that cover the systemization of referral programs I'd highly encourage you to read.

Speaker Bureaus

If you're a keynote speaker, then speaker bureaus can be a possible source of ongoing speaking engagements. Like anything in life, there are pros and cons to using speaker bureaus. First, unless your speaking fee is $10K or above, it can be challenging to get them to even represent you. Speaker bureaus make their money by taking 20%–30% of your fee for getting you the engagement. They tend to push their higher priced speakers because they make more money from booking them.

I saw a stat recently where a particular speaker bureau boasted of having vetted some 16,000 speakers. However, on their site they listed only 750 of them. That's just 4.6% of the speakers. So, even though you've been vetted by them you had less than a one in twenty chance they'll even show you to the event planners they serve.

Social Media

You don't have to look very far to find someone touting the latest social media platform as their greatest source of new leads for their speaking business. If you took them all at their word, then you'll be simultaneously trying to master Facebook, LinkedIn, TikTok, Instagram, Snapchat, Twitter, YouTube, Pinterest and more.

The key is for you to figure out where your largest target audience is primarily hanging out. If you have a team that can keep you active on multiple platforms, then great, go for it. But, if you're a solopreneur, you are better off focusing your efforts on just two or three of them.

Consistently providing high-quality, relevant content to your followers is necessary to keep them engaged, and to keep you front and center in their minds. Regardless of what social media platform(s) you're playing on, your goal is always to get them off social media and to your personal website so you can capture their email address and proactively market to them your products and services.

Building Your Own List

In order to build your own list of followers, you must give people an incentive to get them onto your list. Whether you call it a bribe, a lead magnet, or something else, it's all about an exchange—a quid pro quo. In exchange for giving you their email address, you need to provide them something that they find of value.

Could be a checklist, a special report, a preview chapter of your upcoming book, an audio interview or any one of dozens of other things. What would you have found to be of value when you were getting started in your niche?

Building your own email marketing list is essential for the long-term success of your speaking business.

Media Kit

When you're driving people off social media to your own website, you obviously need to be driving them to a professional looking site with a well-developed media kit. While some are capable of doing it themselves, you'll need to decide if website development is one of those tasks you want to master and take on yourself.

Whether you're a do-it-yourselfer or you're paying an outsider to do it for you, the site needs to "sell" you and your speaking capabilities. Your website should have a comprehensive media kit and/or pressroom and should have all the information necessary for a meeting planner to assess whether you're a good fit for their audience.

Your media kit could include any of the following:

- Introduction
- Fifty- and 100-word bios
- Contact information
- Books published
- Suggested interview questions
- Press ready pictures
- Videos of you in action
- Links to articles you're written
- Speaker one sheet
- Fee schedule
- Listing of previous speaking engagements
- Testimonials from event planners
- Testimonials for attendees
- Scope of services
- Media appearances
- Social media contact information
- Your tech requirements

Networking and Other Resources

Being seen regularly by others in the industry is important. Attend virtual summits even if you're not speaking at them. Contribute meaningful content to other's events or their blogs. Find podcasts that you can make guest appearances on.

For a list of current online resources that can help you land speaking gigs, visit BuildaProfitableSpeakingBusiness.com/resources.

Pay to Play Speaking Opportunities

Some live and virtual events offer sponsorship opportunities where, as part of your sponsorship, you are given a speaking slot either on the main stage or in a breakout session.

These can cost anywhere from a couple hundred to a few thousand dollars depending on the event. If you're good at selling from the platform and an event is a good fit for you in terms of the number of attendees and the demographics of the audience then it could be well worth your while to step up as a sponsor.

Bottom line, regardless of which method(s) you utilize to get speaking engagements <u>you must be proactive</u>. Go out and get it!

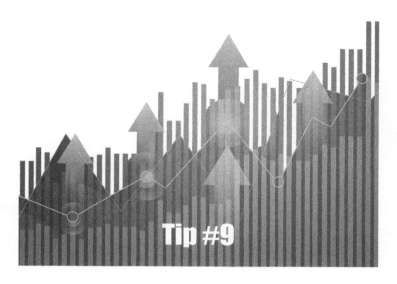

Tip #9

Repurposing Your Assets

When you deliver a speech to, for example, ABC Corporation and you're then contracted to deliver the same content to XYZ Corporation do you write an entire new speech from scratch? In almost all cases I'd say the answer is no. You take your same presentation that you should tweak a little bit for the new client, but it's essentially the same speech.

What you are doing is repurposing your existing content for another audience. Having to start from scratch every time is a real killer of productivity and the profitability of your speaking business.

But it's not just your speeches you need to repurpose. All the content that you should be creating for your social media channels—whether it's Facebook, LinkedIn, Instagram, Twitter, Snapchat, TikTok, YouTube, Pinterest or any other platform—should be content that you've leveraged by repurposing.

There's no doubt that a lot of your success as a speaker will depend largely on your ability to attract and engage followers. The more people that you have in your sphere of influence should translate into a greater number of speaking engagements.

Should you be on every social media platform? By and large, no. You should focus your efforts on the two to three platforms where your ideal prospects are hanging out. Now, if you have a team that is handling your social media (whether it's an internal or external team doesn't matter) then you may be able to be present on more platforms without burning yourself out individually.

The key to success on these social media platforms is regularly posting valuable content. Only you can determine what schedule is right for you—whether that's daily, weekly or something else. Whatever it is—consistency is vitally important.

So, let's talk a bit more about repurposing your content. If you've created a video for your YouTube channel what else can you do with that video?

- Take a snippet of that video to use on TikTok or as a YouTube Short
- Post the actual video or a link to the video on your blog
- Pull the audio from the video and put it out on the various podcast platforms
- Transcribe the video and use it to create an article for your blog or the beginnings of a chapter for your new book
- Pull pithy quotes from the video to use as tweets for Twitter
- Post a form of that content to your LinkedIn account if you have one

You get the idea. One piece of content, with multiple uses in one format or another applied across many platforms.

Remember, you can outsource your social media efforts. Only you can decide when the time is right for that. And don't hesitate to take advantage of tools like Hootsuite, Sprout or Loomly, social media managing sites that allow you to post across multiple platforms simultaneously.

Bottom line, your ability to repurpose content is an important aspect of building an even bigger platform for you and your speaking business. Anything you're able to do that will help you leverage what you've already created will help you immensely. REPURPOSE. YOUR. CONTENT.

Your Ability to Repurpose Content is an Important Aspect of
Building a Bigger Platform For Your Speaking Business

Outsourcing

One of the biggest challenges most speakers face is deciding when to let go of a particular task needed to run their business. They're afraid that somebody else won't be able to do it as well as them and, as a result, feel they absolutely have to do it themselves.

When your speaking business is starting out, you will probably find you're wearing many or all of these hats:

- Travel planner
- Speech writer
- Social media poster
- Marketing manager

- Public speaker
- Shipping manager
- Customer service manager
- Order taker
- Website developer and maintainer
- And many more!

Let me ask you this. What do you really value your time at? Is it $10 an hour, $20, $50, $100, $250, $500, more?

Let's assume you feel your time is worth $250 per hour. That means if you're spending your time doing $10 or $20 or even $50 per hour tasks, then you're probably not spending your time as wisely as you should.

You need to focus your energies on tasks only you can truly do. This means the public speaking and speech writing should be at the top and primary focus of your to-do list. If you're spending your time on lower value tasks, then you are stunting the growth of your speaking business and, as a result, the long-term profitability of your business.

I know of speakers who spend an hour or more per day packing up their own book orders and fighting traffic to get to the post office in time rather than outsourcing that task to a fulfillment company.

When it comes to the decision to outsource, be honest with yourself about what you're good at and what you enjoy. A good friend of mine, Alex Mandossian, once told me to "Pay others to do what you have to work at, but they play at." In other words, you're throwing money away if you continue doing things someone else could do more efficiently.

Now, if there's a task you're good at and it brings great joy to you, then go ahead and do it. Know that, in terms of the growth of your speaking business, it will probably hurt you some in the long run. But life's about balance and you deserve pleasure.

I have another friend who's a multi-millionaire internet marketer who continues to design his own graphics because he enjoys it so much. Sure, he recognizes he could pay someone else to do it for far less than what his time is worth, but he doesn't want to give up the enjoyment it brings him.

Virtual assistants (VAs) are an important part of many speakers' teams. If you feel you're ready to hire a VA, then it's up to you to determine which tasks you could assign to someone else. You'll also have to decide whether you want to use a U.S. based or international virtual assistant. There are pros and cons to each, and only you can determine which will be the best fit for you.

International VAs are usually considerably less expensive. Personally, I've had good success utilizing VAs based in the Philippines, although I did have to work around the time difference and a few other factors. A quick online search of pros vs. cons of U.S. vs. international VAs will help you formulate the questions you need to ask yourself to determine which is best for you.

Controlling Your Speaking Environment

To maximize your effectiveness as a speaker, it is of paramount importance that you control the environment in which you will be speaking as much as possible. Your environment can certainly include things like the room temperature and lighting. But it will also include a lot of other factors you may have not considered previously.

Anything that can influence your onstage performance falls under the classification of your environment. Some may be considered major and others minor, but all can affect how well your message is received by the audience and, if you are selling from the platform, how well you sell. We're talking about things like:

- Sound quality
- Your introduction
- Internet connections
- Clicker
- Banging doors
- Q & A sessions
- Testimonials from the audience
- Intro and exit music

Sound Quality

I have seen too many speakers show up too close to the scheduled start of their presentation. So, the audio crew is slapping a microphone on them at the last minute and there is not enough time to do a proper soundcheck prior to the speaker taking stage. And then they wonder why the audio quality sucks during their presentation.

That is why you should get to an event well in advance of any scheduled presentation. If you speak before lunch, find out when the audio crew will be in the room, either the night before or the morning of your scheduled presentation so a proper soundcheck can be done. If you speak after lunch, then check things out during the lunch break. If you're using a lapel microphone, find out specifically where on your clothing you should affix the microphone for best sound.

Walk the stage once you are mic'd up to check for spots you should avoid during your presentation. These are the spots where interference occurs and the audience would get a loud "shriek" or other earsplitting sound that will detract from your presentation. Know the "hot spots" going in and you will have a better sounding presentation throughout your speech.

Internet Connection

Never ever ever ever do a presentation where you are relying on a live internet connection to show something to the audience. This is one of those things in your environment you have very little control over. I have seen too many presentations ruined by a lost or very slow internet connection. You are taking an unnecessary chance anytime you try to go live online.

The way you can control this factor is to use screen-shots from the web in your presentation rather than the live shot. It works just as well, and you don't run the risk of looking the fool with connectivity issues. Internet connections in meeting rooms can also be very expensive—hundreds of dollars per day. So, you may also be asking the event promoter to incur an additional expense just for you that could have been avoided.

Clicker

Another seemingly minor factor that can cause you major headaches is the simple clicker. If you are utilizing a PowerPoint in your presentation, you will likely use a wireless clicker. Before your presentation, be sure to test the clicker so you fully understand its range and exactly where you should point it when you are ready to advance to your next slide.

Banging Doors

A smart event promoter usually tries to control audience access to the meeting room through a pre-selected set of doors. They do this for several reasons. For one, it's more effective to greet audience members if they are entering through only one set of doors. Another reason is it enables them to force the crowd to pass by the sales table whenever they are exiting the room.

It's inevitable that people will enter or exit the room during your presentation. If the door bangs noisily every time it is shut, it can be a major distraction to the participants. You want them focusing their attention on you and not turning to see who is coming in or going out every time they hear the door.

There are a couple of low-tech solutions you can suggest to an event promoter if you see the doors could be a problem. First, you can suggest they tape the push bar of the exit door(s) shut. This does not hinder exit access in any way, but it does silence the noisy push bar that people hear when the door is being opened.

But then the door closes, sometimes with a loud bang. So, the second thing you can suggest is simply throwing a towel over the top of the door to cushion things when the door shuts. Eliminating these two potential distractions can help you to better control your environment.

Q & A Sessions

Should you take questions during your presentation? In all but rare cases I would say no. Turning control of the microphone over to someone in the audience is one of the quickest ways to lose control of your presentation. Invite them to meet you at the sales table if they have any questions or to come and talk with you during a break.

You should already have a sense of what questions people will ask you about your topic, and you should have the answers to the questions you are most frequently asked already worked into your presentation.

Testimonials from the Audience

Like Q & A sessions, soliciting testimonials from the audience about your products or services is an area fraught with potential problems. First, you must alert the event promoter ahead of time if it's necessary to have a microphone available to the audience. Otherwise, you can have a few awkward moments of silence while they are scrambling around for a microphone.

Even if you have made all the arrangements in advance, you are still turning over control of your room to someone else when you give them a microphone. I've seen testimonials get totally out of control and last way too long. Sometimes it is hard to wrestle back control of the microphone.

If you are going to use live testimonials, you must carefully choose who you are going to use. Give them clear guidelines on how much time they will have when you go to them for their testimonial and make sure you know what they are going to be saying ahead of time so you don't get any unexpected surprises.

Intro and Exit Music

Music can have a powerful impact on people. Properly selected music played as you are getting ready to take the stage or when you have just finished and are exiting the stage can help you to create some real excitement in the room. You can help by selecting music you feel best fits with your presentation. A smart promoter will be more than happy to accommodate your musical requests.

In Conclusion

There are some factors in your environment you may have little or no control over, such as the room temperature and event lighting. But you can see there are a number of other factors you may exercise some control over.

The Better You Control Your Speaking Environment, the Greater Your Chances for Success.

Tip #12

Your Stage Introduction

Should you pre-write the introduction you want the event emcee or whoever will be introducing you to the audience to read? In a word—yes. Does that mean every person who does your intro over the course of your speaking career will read it word for word? Of course not.

But if you do not have something for the emcee to follow and they "wing" it, who knows what you're going to get. So, write something out and get it to the proper person in advance so they can at least familiarize themselves with what they will be saying about you.

If a colleague has done a great job of introducing you at a previous event, then the event promoter may let that person do your intro rather than the event emcee. If the audience already knows, likes and trusts your colleague, that can be a fantastic idea. But if your colleague is someone they won't be familiar with, you are better off utilizing the event emcee.

Regardless of who will be doing your intro, do NOT make it a complete autobiography. I have seen many speakers lose their audience before they ever uttered their first word on stage. How? With an introduction that went on and on and on and on and on. You get the idea.

Many speakers think they need to tout their credentials on stage much more than necessary. The audience is interested in what is in it for them. The minutes you spend on how wonderful you are and the great things you've done just doesn't do it for them. The fact that you are on the stage in the first place pretty much provides you most of the credentials you need.

And if I hear another speaker say, "I don't say this to impress you, but rather to impress upon you…" I might be sick. A two- or three-minute introduction is more than enough, and the primary focus should be on what your audience is going to learn, not on how great you are. Some speakers have gone to video introductions to exercise maximum control over their introductions. You will have to decide if this is right for you.

Offers from Stage

I f you are a "free" speaker (platform seller) vs. a "fee" speaker (keynoter) that means your income will be directly related to your effectiveness in selling from the platform.

I've seen speakers deliver great content and then freeze up when it came to the sales close portion of their presentation. I've also seen speakers deliver poor content and then do great when they got to their close.

Your objective is to obviously do both—deliver great content and then do a great sales job from the platform. Remember, your first responsibility is to your audience and your obligation is to deliver them great content. In a typical presentation, at least 80% of your time should be spent on content and 20% or less on your close.

That means in a ninety-minute presentation, roughly the first seventy-five minutes should be spent teaching and only in the last fifteen will you do any selling. Of course, you are "selling" yourself through the course of your presentation by sharing your expertise in a way that makes them want to learn more from you. The reaction you are looking for is something like, "Man, if what he's teaching us here for free is this good, his other stuff must really be great!"

The transition from the content portion of your presentation to the sales portion of your presentation should be seamless. I've heard too many speakers change their tone or pace when they got to their close and not even recognize that they were doing it. And, believe me, the audience hears it, too. You can just feel the barriers immediately go up when the crowd feels they are being sold to.

The entire dynamics of a presentation change when you are selling at the end of your presentation rather than delivering content only. Some speakers can get on stage all day long and share content, but ask them to sell something at the end and it makes them squeamish.

It does take time and practice to make that smooth transition from content to close. But there are a lot of other things going on that you will want to pay close attention to.

As you watch other speakers selling from the platform, take notice of what they are doing. Here are just some of the things you should be watching closely:

- How do they handle their transition?
- What do they include in their offer?
- Is their offer simple or complex?
- Are they offering multiple options?
- Do they pass out order forms or direct people to the sales table?
- Do they utilize a single- or two-step closing process?
- Are they selling digital or physical goods, or some combination of both?
- Are they delivering their product right at the event?
- What is the price point of their offer?
- Are they offering payment plans?
- What sort of guarantee, if any, are they offering?

Let's dive into each of these questions with a bit more detail. We have already talked about the transition, so let's move on to the offer related questions.

First, you will need to decide what it is you are going to sell from the platform. Will you sell one-on-one coaching, group coaching, a physical product, a webinar or teleseminar series, or some combination of these things? There is no wrong or right answer. I've seen all variations sold very effectively from the platform.

You certainly want to create a compelling offer. But, from my experience, it is much more about the quality of the content you deliver and the rapport you establish with your audience that leads to back-of-the-room success than anything else. You can pretty much bundle anything together and have a "winner" if you are a great speaker and can effectively manage your close.

Some speakers adhere to the "more is better" philosophy and stack on item after item into their offer. They present a total value of some gigantic amount, and then they do price drop after price drop until they reach their actual selling price. It seems to them like it should be a no-brainer to take their offer because they are giving you so much for relatively so little.

I have seen this approach work great and I've also seen it fail miserably. If the value to price proposition seems to be out of whack, then it may seem unbelievable to the audience and you can come across as the stereotypical used car salesman.

And, if you are speaking at a multi-speaker event and some of the speakers that preceded you during the event used a similar closing technique as you, then your "But wait, there's more" may come across as copycatish and as a bit of a joke.

One thing most speakers don't do well that could significantly improve their performance is to find out what all the other speakers sharing that stage will be speaking about and what they will be offering. Then, try to be different. I'm not saying don't be authentic. I'm saying that if they sell a price X then you may want to sell at price Y. If they are going to offer A, B and C in their offer, you may want to offer X, Y and Z. If they are offering only a digital product, then you offer a physical product. Be different.

I have been at events where the promoter had three different people speak about copywriting. If you were the third speaker in that group, what would you do to differentiate yourself? If you are the third one offering a $2,000 package of copywriting training and resources, then the attractiveness of your offer will be much lower because the audience has already "been there, done that" in their mind.

Only over time, by testing different offers, will you get a true feel of what works best for you. Do you do better at a $497 price point, a $997 price point or a $1997 price point. Or more? Do you sell better if you offer a physical product they can take right with them from the event, or with a digital-only delivery through a membership site? Do you do better if you offer payment plans or not?

Do you sell better offering a single package or with good, better and best options? There is a continuing hot debate on this question. Some say, "A confused mind never buys," and others say the more options you give them the better are your chances of getting them to buy something. Only through testing will you find out what works best for you.

Do you sell better if you pass out order forms to the audience near the end of your presentation or if you just direct them to the sales table to get an order form? If you are selling a high-ticket coaching program, do you do better with a single- or two-step process?

You can see all the variables involved in the sales process. You need to continually test and tweak your closes to determine which combination of options pulls the best for you over time. Keep honing and improving, and watch your sales success grow!

Tip #14

Harvesting Their List

One of the quickest ways to get yourself uninvited from appearing on future stages by event promoters is to gain a reputation as a person who is only there to capture the names and email addresses of all the attendees.

This is known as "harvesting the list"—offering something for free or at very low cost during a presentation and encouraging the participants to go to a certain website and provide their name and email in exchange for something of value.

There may or may not be an offer at the end of the presentation for a high-ticket item.

Event promoters work very hard to get people into their events and seriously frown on obvious attempts to simply name capture. If you're even considering something like this (in my opinion, you shouldn't) then you must absolutely discuss it in advance with the event promoter and get his or her approval.

Perhaps you can make an agreement whereby the promoter knows they'll receive their share of any backend sales that occur after an event from those names that you capture at an event. Honestly, they're a bit leery to do this because essentially, you're on the honor system and they have no great way to monitor it.

A straight harvesting of the list is one of the most highly unwelcome acts a speaker can pull on a promoter. Don't do it!

Upsells and Undervaluing

attended an event a while back and ran across a speaker I have known for several years as a keynote speaker only. Let's call him Ted for the purposes of this story. Ted was excited because he had finally completed his first product he could sell from the platform, and he realized he would not have to rely only on his speaking fee to generate income.

When Ted got on the stage, he wowed the audience and his product was really in hot demand at the back-of-the-room sales table. He probably sold 20% of the audience on his program, which he had every right to be happy about.

But then I noticed the event promoter over to the side of the sales table kind of slowly shaking her head. She did not say anything to Ted immediately, but I was pretty sure I knew exactly why she was shaking her head because I've seen it many times myself at other events.

Ted had done a fantastic presentation. The audience had really responded well to his content and then to his end of talk offer for his product. So, he had a hungry crowd lined up at the back table to spend money on his offer. So that is what he sold them—his $197 course.

What I'm sure the promoter was shaking her head about what that Ted seemed to have no grasp of the concept of an upsell.

What is an Upsell?

An upsell is the offer of an additional product or service at the time someone is placing their order. The most well-known example of this that people can relate to is the "Would you like fries with that?" line you get at McDonald's™ when you order a sandwich. They know a large percentage of the people will say yes and they will make additional profit from that customer on that transaction.

In the world of selling from the platform, it is when the customer is at the sales table in the back and they're already pulled out their credit card and are placing an order for your product or service. What additional product or service could you offer them that would be of great value to them?

If you truly have additional products or services that could improve their situation, you are, in reality, doing your customers a disservice by not shining a light on these additional products

Upsells are very popular in the online world. When you are going through the online checkout process, you will frequently see a message pop up to the effect of "since you are buying Product A today you are eligible to also receive Product B for just X, a savings of Y versus buying the products separately." You then have the option of adding that item to your shopping cart or not.

I have seen upsells online work so well that 95% of the people took the upsell. I have also seen situations where the product offered as an upsell was priced at five times the price of the original product offered. And it worked very well. What you can upsell is really only limited by your own creativity.

Think about infomercials. The $9.97 gadget you initially ordered typically turns into a $60 sale because of the upsells that they do when you call in to place your order.

So, what can you upsell during a live event at the sales table? Remember, they are already in a buying mood, so take advantage of that positive momentum and offer them something additional.

Possible Upsells for the Platform Speaker

- Follow-up webinar series
- Follow-up teleseminar series
- Group coaching calls
- One-on-one coaching calls

- Q & A calls
- Additional USBs/CD/DVD/workbooks
- Tickets to your own live event
- Access to a membership site

It is sometimes a challenge to determine what you should include in your main offer from stage. What should the core offer be? What items should be bonuses? And what products or services should be part of your upsell? It is one of those things you will only determine the best answer to by testing different variations over time.

Avoid Upsell Hell

Just be sure to avoid what I call "Upsell Hell." Upsell Hell is where you almost beat your customer to death with upsell after upsell after upsell after upsell. Just because they have said yes to your first upsell does not mean you want to keep going until they say no. Again, you should test. But if you are going to keep pushing until you get pushback, you risk upsetting your customers and destroying the goodwill and relationship you have worked so hard to build

Training the Back-of-the-Room Crew

Of course, if you are going to offer an upsell at the back-of-the-room sales table at a live event, it is critical you provide the proper training on how to do that upsell to the sales table staff. If you are bringing your own assistant or staff to help at the sales table, that's great—most event promoters will welcome the help.

But if the crew is provided entirely by the event promoter, it is important to remember they will probably be working with multiple speakers over the course of the event and are dealing with multiple offers. The offers all start to blend together after a while, and they can become confused. So, you probably should not make your upsell overly complex or they will not do a great job of helping you sell it.

Provide a Written Summary Sheet

You should also have a good written summary of both your basic offer and a separate summary sheet for your upsell. People frequently get confused about what they have bought and if you give them a nice written piece after their purchase that summarizes what they are receiving you will have happier customers and reduce customer service burdens for yourself.

Remember, people will gladly pay good money for products and services that provide real value and the solution they are looking for. Do not undervalue the worth of what you have to offer people, which is another common mistake many speakers make.

Don't Undervalue What You Have to Offer

I am sure the event promoter in our story was also shaking her head about Ted's $197 price point. This is a fairly low price point, and event promoters generally want people that can sell from the stage and put money into their pockets. The back-of-the-room sales are where most promoters make their money. If you are selling a low-ticket item, it just does not add up to much for the promoter after the normal 50/50 split of your sales.

Look at your price point. Like anything, you need to test and see what works best, but price points of $997, $1997 and $2997 or higher are common at many events. Do not be afraid to test higher price points. If necessary, figure out what you can bundle together to justify a higher price point.

So, do not undervalue and do upsell.

Tip #16

Selling Products in Development

If memory serves me correctly, the event was in Los Angeles and the attendance was somewhere around 400 people. Our back of the room crew was primed and ready to go, and then it happened. That table rush that every speaker selling from the platform dreams of was happening right before his eyes!

Dozens upon dozens of people rushed the table to place their order for his latest "magic blue pill" solution to website development. Our team processed sale after sale, and when all was said and done, this one speaker had generated nearly $375,000 in sales. It was definitely a day to remember.

But then there was a slight problem. Well, maybe not slight—significant would be a better word. The promised software solution that the speaker's team was putting the finishing touches on didn't work. For whatever reason, they couldn't fix the issue and every single sale had to be refunded—all $375,000 worth.

It was humiliating for the speaker, and financially devastating for both the speaker and the event promoter.

Unfortunately, this scenario played out again a year or two later at another event our team was handling in Vancouver, British Columbia. This time the speaker sold a product that was also in the developmental stage, and he stated that the product would be ready in a week or so. Invariably, a week turned into two weeks, and then into four. All those attendees that had purchased his product requested a refund. Fortunately, it wasn't to the tune of $375,000 again, but it still ended up with the speaker having a lot of egg on his face, and it created embarrassment and some financial challenges for the event promoter.

I've found that, over the course of my business career, that this timing pretty much runs true. If you think something is going to take a week, then it takes two. If you think it's going to take two, then it'll be three to four. Do you agree?

Now, you've probably heard people talk about following the concept of sell it first and then develop it if it sells. And, for a coaching program, training program, or webinar series I think that's fine. Creating the content as you go has been a very successful approach for many speakers.

Just be sure you're able to deliver what you promise to your students in the timeframes that you've promised.

In my opinion, selling any product or service that's in development is a very dangerous game to play. If you're unable to deliver, it's embarrassing for you, and it could be a financial nightmare in both the short-term and the long-term.

Why the long-term? Well, let me ask you this. How many event promoters are going to invite you back to their stage when they've had that kind of experience with you? And remember, promoters talk, so word will get around about what happened.

I personally recommend never selling a product or service that isn't fully developed (with the exception of content delivery). There may be those that disagree with me, but first-hand experience has shown me the dangers of going down that path.

Tip #17

Who's Handling the Money?

I f you're a speaker who will be making your living primarily by selling from the stage, then it is critical that you understand how the money will be handled at an event. The company I founded, Speaker Fulfillment Services, got its start managing the back sales table at various internet and information marketing conferences.

These were multi-speaker events over the course of three or four days, and we'd provide the crew and the merchant account that could handle multiple speakers and a large amount of money in a short period of time. Back in the early 2000s, it was nearly impossible to obtain a merchant account that would allow you to process multiple speakers so our services were in high demand. Especially if you were going to need to process several hundred thousand dollars or more at an event.

We'd take care of all the money management for sales at an event. We'd pay the speakers and the promoter and take a cut of the promoter's portion for providing the service. If a speaker was offering a payment plan, we'd set up and process all the deferred sales and pay the speaker and promoter their shares once they were processed.

But bringing in a third party to handle all the sales is just one of three possible money management models I've seen used at an event. The others are:

1. The promoter runs all the sales through their own merchant account and then pays the speaker their portion. Typically at a selling event, it is a 50/50 split between the speaker and the event promoter.
2. The speakers process their own sales and are responsible for then submitting to the event promoter their portion.

If an event promoter will allow you to process your own sales, I'd highly encourage you to do so—to be the one who is in control of your own money. But they may insist on being the one who handles all the processing so they can know exactly how much each of their speakers has sold.

When you are processing your own sales, be sure you have your own merchant account set up properly. When you set up a merchant account, you'll specify what types of good and services you'll be selling, what your average ticket price will be and how much you usually expect to process in a month.

If you plan to do your own processing at a speaking event, and you expect to sell significantly more than what you've set as your usual guidelines with your merchant account provider, it is critical that you communicate with them in advance. A sudden surge in the amount of processing sends up all sorts of red flags for a processor and could lead to your merchant account being shut down.

I've found that if they know what is going on beforehand, they won't have any problem with the larger than normal volume.

Several years ago, I had a client who was doing a new product launch. They opened their cart and the sales began to come in. Then suddenly, midway through the first afternoon, they had their merchant account shut off. Why? Because they hadn't informed their provider that they were going to be doing a new product launch. I estimate conservatively that this failure to communicate cost them between $300,000 and $400,000 in sales. Ouch!

If the promoter or a third party will be processing all the sales, be sure you understand the exact terms and conditions related to the payout of monies. In fact, this should be spelled out in the contract you have with an event promoter.

Usually, an initial payout of money will transpire around thirty to thirty-five days after an event has ended.

Whoever is processing needs to account for any possible returns and doesn't want to pay out money and then have to try and collect it back because someone decided they wanted a refund.

Keep in mind that, if you are offering a payment plan, some of your payments will be deferred. Credit cards can expire and sometimes it can be challenging to collect all the money from a sale. I recommend never offering more than three or four payments on a product purchase. Any longer than that and it becomes a nightmare to keep track of everything over that longer period of time.

If a promoter is going to allow you to process your own sales, you are on your honor to pay them in a timely manner. I've seen promoters shafted by speakers and speakers shafted by promoters, so watch yourself. One of the quickest ways to get yourself uninvited from appearing on anybody's stage is to gain a reputation as someone who doesn't honor their commitments.

This includes the scenario where somebody who attended an event contacts you just after the event and wants to purchase whatever product or service you offered. If you get that sale, you are honor bound to give the promoter their portion even if the sale occurred post event.

Who's handling the money is an important question for any event you'll be speaking at. Be sure you know how it will be handled in advance of every speaking engagement.

Prima Donnas

'**ve** heard it more than once from an event promoter. "Man, this guy is a pain in the ass to deal with. He won't be coming back to my platform in the future." What would cause an event promoter to feel this way? Two words—prima donna.

What makes a speaker a prima donna? It's the speaker who seemingly has demand after demand and expects to be treated differently than every other speaker on the agenda. It's the guy who insists on having only green M&Ms in a bowl on the stage (yes, that's really happened).

It's the lady who must have a very specific brand of bottled sparkling water chilled to exactly 57.6 degrees or the guy who demands to have a chauffeured limousine pick him up and drop him off at the airport at the proper time.

It's the speaker who doesn't tell the promoter he's having product shipped in on a pallet and then shows up and expects the promoter to drop everything to get his products delivered, assembled and packaged in the meeting room.

It's the speaker who shows up with a full entourage and expects the event promoter to comp them tickets to the event and arrange special seating for them.

Or maybe it's the guy who you've graciously provided a room for because you had a few comped rooms in your room block, who then runs up a gigantic room service bill for food and alcohol.

It could be the lady who makes changes to the sales split in your contract with her and tries to sneak it by you.

Or the guy who ignores the large countdown clock in the back of the room and runs over on his time by twenty minutes and then, to boot, because he isn't happy with his sales, begs the promoter for an additional few minutes before the end of the event to do another pitch from stage.

The speaking industry is a large one, but it's also a fairly close-knit group. Event promoters talk to each other and, if you're that prima donna who's a pain to deal with, the word will get around. And while you might get on someone's stage once and even maybe sell very well, the promoter probably won't invite you back to his or her stage again because they just don't want to have to deal with you.

Talk about a major hit to the long-term profitability of your speaking business!

If you have any special requests for an event promoter, you should always make them well in advance of the event. If you're a keynote speaker, then the person or organization who brings you in will typically cover your air fare, hotel, food and transportation.

Main thing is there shouldn't be any surprises for the promoter—they should know up front what they're getting into when working with you. If you can negotiate that chauffeured limo, great. But to expect to be treated differently than every other speaker is simply not the way to go.

A humble "I'm here to help" attitude goes a long way to being the kind of speaker an event promoter will want to deal with. You're in it for the long haul, so cultivate and nurture your relationships with those who are running an event. You'll have much greater success over your career it you are one of those speakers the event promoters love to bring to their stage.

Hit and Run Speakers

One of my biggest pet peeves in the speaking industry is that of the hit and run speaker. It's the guy or gal who literally swoops in just a couple of minutes before their scheduled time and is out the door just as soon as he or she has finished speaking.

Now, I get it that sometimes there are scheduling issues that make this a necessary scenario. But if this is a regular occurrence for a speaker, it is so unfair to an event promoter. They're wondering "Is he going to show? Is he not going to show? What am I going to do if he doesn't show?" You're creating undue stress on that promoter who probably won't be inclined to have you back on their stage again. And who would blame them?

It can also create issues for an audio crew because they're hurrying to get you mic'd up at the very last minute.

You also have these other possible negatives

- No opportunity to really get any kind of feel for the audience.
- No opportunity to meet other speakers who are promoters themselves and have their own events.
- You've not heard any of the other speakers, so you can't build upon anything they taught or avoid an outright duplication of some of their content.
- If you're using a PowerPoint or other presentation, there's no time to do a check to make sure everything plays properly.

If you take off immediately after your speaking slot, it doesn't give you a chance to further build upon any rapport with the audience during your time on stage. It will most likely, if you're selling from the platform, cost you sales because you're not there to answer questions from attendees.

And it's not just in person events where this can be an issue. If you're participating in any type of virtual summit or live webcast, you should be logged in and ready to go a minimum of ten minutes before your scheduled starting time. I've hosted so many trainings and other events where

I've been wondering up to the last minute whether the other person is going to show or not.

Putting on any kind of event is stressful enough for an event promoter. Don't be the one who adds to the stress by showing up at the very last minute. And don't hit the door so quickly after your talk that you're not available to mingle with the attendees. You have a responsibility to the event promoter to help make those attending an event feel that their experience was a very positive one.

Now, should the situation arise where you absolutely must "hit and run" an event, then proper communication with both the event promoter and audience is critical. A clear explanation of what is going on along with a sincere apology can go a long way. If you must leave the venue immediately, apologize to the audience and make sure they know you're available for questions via email or by scheduling a consultation time with you.

Best case scenario—avoid becoming a hit and run speaker altogether.

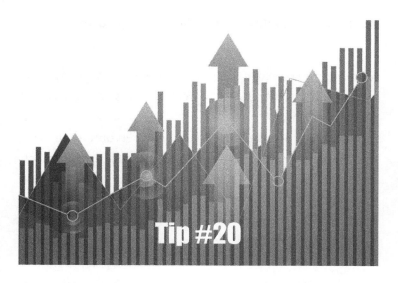

Tip #20

Having a Book

There is little doubt that one of the quickest ways to establish yourself as an expert is to be an author. Make no mistake about it—being a speaker is great. When you add in the fact that you're also the author of a book on your subject, it can multiply your credibility tenfold.

Speakers and authors both hold a special position in the eye of the general public. In their mind, if you are a public speaker and you have written a book, then you must be the real deal and someone worthy of notice.

Your book can be a great lead source for your higher ticket coaching programs and live events. For just a small amount, a person can learn more about you and what you have to offer. Or it can be a great business card for you in many situations.

Yet many speakers can't seem to overcome their writer's block or whatever is holding them back from completing their first book. Writing a book need not be difficult, and the benefits you will gain from having that book will make it all worthwhile.

Many people think that the only way you can write a book is to sit down with a blank sheet of paper or blank computer screen and start adding words to the page. This is certainly one way to write a book, and many do it in exactly this manner. To keep themselves on task they have daily or weekly writing goals that continue to push them toward the completion of their book.

But starting with a blank sheet of paper is certainly not the only way one can write a book. If you are having trouble getting going on your book here are some alternative ways to write your book.

1. Speak your book. If you are a great talker but not such a great writer, just get a decent microphone and recording software and say what you want to write. Of course, it will need some editing, but speaking your book is a great way to get your thoughts into writing.

   Just bear in mind that one hour of audio typically translate into about thirty-five pages of transcript. So, if you goal is to have a 150-page book then you are going to need about four-and-a-half to five hours of audio to transcribe.

2. Record video of yourself at a live event and have it transcribed to form the basis for your book.

3. Combine a series of articles you have previously written and organize it appropriately, and you have a book.

4. Combine a bunch of blog posts you have done over the last couple years together to form the basis for your book.

5. Have someone do a series of interviews with you and use the transcription of those interviews to make a book.

6. If necessary, start with a compilation book with other authors where you are contributing one chapter only to the book to get started.

7. Take an existing home study course or other product you have written previously and pull content from that to write your book. Repurposing is a key phrase you need to understand. You don't have to necessarily reinvent the wheel—you may already have content you can reuse in some form as the basis for your book.

8. Hire a ghostwriter to write your book for you.

However you get it done, get it done. Your book is an important weapon in your marketing arsenal, and in helping you build your platform as a speaker.

It should be a key component of your physical media kit. You will want to send it to event promoters on whose stage you want to speak.

Another key component to helping you build your platform as a speaker is ensuring the quality of your book is outstanding. Even the best content will go unnoticed if you do not put your book together in a way that encourages the end reader to read it cover to cover. In other words, it is all about product consumption.

So how do you make your book more consumable for the reader? I recently went into a local bookstore and picked up a book in the business section on marketing that sounded kind of interesting based on the title.

I began thumbing through it, and the first chapter went on for not ten, not twenty, but thirty-five pages! My thought was, "If it's going to be this much work to get through just the first chapter, then I don't even want to start reading this book."

People like to consume information in bite-sized chunks. When you overwhelm them with lengthy chapters, you make it nearly impossible for the reader to feel that intermittent sense of accomplishment that comes from completing a chapter. So, the answer is obvious. Divide your chapters into more reasonable consumable segments—a maximum of seven to ten pages per chapter.

Make sure your paragraphs aren't overly long. Each should be two to three sentences in most cases. Overly long paragraphs intimidate the reader and stifle consumption.

Utilize pull quotes, boxed case studies, bulleted lists, illustrations, graphs, charts and other things that help break up the page so that everything is not pure text. Bottom line, if you make it easier on the eye, you make it easier for the reader to consume.

Avoid teeny tiny font that is difficult to read. Most book layout people use a minimum of eleven-point font so that those of us with older eyes can see the page better. If your subject is aimed at baby boomers, then you are kidding yourself if you think you can go with ten-point type or smaller to save on page count. Most probably won't read it.

You must have a book. Preferably, several books. For a typical non-fiction book, you want to limit the total page count to somewhere between 150–225 pages. Go much longer and you reintroduce that factor of overwhelm into the equation.

You may not be able to include everything you know about a subject in a single book. That's okay. You're better off breaking your knowledge into two or more books if you have enough material than trying to include it all in one and have your book be too long.

Remember, it's all about consumption. If you get them to read your book, then the chances of them coming to you for other products and/or services you may offer goes up dramatically.

Always be sure to include in your book several "bounce back" mechanisms. These are ways you can capture the reader's information to follow up with them via autoresponders or offline methods.

When someone buys your book in a traditional retail bookstore or online, then you do not receive that buyer information. So, the inclusion of some bribe within your book (preferably multiple bribes) to get them to come to your website is important. You can offer some free bonus material or a checklist or anything that they can access only by giving you their contact information. You must have a book. You must have a book. You must have a book.

Tip #21

Leveraging Travel Time

Elsewhere in this book we talked about the number of days typically involved in an on-site speaking engagement. If you recall, that was an average of three days total time on the road for a corporate keynote speaking engagement and up to five days for a multiple speaker conference. That means you've got a lot of time on your hands while you're traveling. What can you do to leverage that time to help you create a more profitable speaking business?

1. Make it your continuing education time. You should never stop learning as a speaker, so use

airport downtime and time aboard planes as your learning time. Catch up on all the podcast episodes related to your industry that you've been meaning to listen to. Read that industry magazine or book you're behind on and have been meaning to finish.

2. Our email inbox never seems to get smaller. Use the time to scroll through your box and answer those things that need to be answered.

3. Create content. Jot down some blog post ideas, or start or continue writing that new book.

4. Market research time.

5. Practice your speech.

6. Start writing that back pocket speech I talked about in another chapter.

7. Write your thank you notes to those you have met at an event. Always carry notecards, envelopes and stamps in your carry on so you can knock this task out before you arrive back at home.

8. Time to review that to-do list. What do you need to delete, add, or reprioritize?

9. Call your mom or dad or sister or brother or children or old college friend. Speaking can be a lonely business and it's important to keep in touch with those who are the reason you do what you do.

10. Consider taking an Uber or Lyft to and from the airport. It may be less expensive than parking your vehicle for a few days and it gives you more time to potentially work on any of the items on this list.

Summary

I hope you've found this book to be highly valuable as you learn more and more about how the speaking industry works. I look forward to our next encounter and wish you the greatest of success with your speaking career!

Please go to Amazon.com and leave your review of the book

About Bret Ridgway

Bret Ridgway is a twenty-five-year veteran of the speaking industry and founded Get.Ship.Done. (formerly known as Speaker Fulfillment Services), a company dedicated to working with authors, speakers and information marketers by providing backend order fulfillment services and production of products "beyond the book." He is author of seven books and a frequent guest at live events speaking on topics for authors and speakers. He can be reached via email at info@BretRidgway.com.

My story—Way back in 1992, I had the fortunate privilege of attending Gary Halbert's "Hurricane Andrew Seminar" in Key West, Florida. Little did I know at the time how that event would change my life and the interesting paths that it would lead me down.

Of course, there were specific things that led me to being in Key West those many years ago, but for the purposes of this story, that's where it all began. Gary Halbert's seminar was my first exposure to the world of direct marketing outside the world of telemarketing, which I had been involved with at that time for about ten years.

But over the course of those few days back in 1992, I had the wonderful opportunity to learn from masters like Gary Halbert, Ted Nicholas, Bill Myers, David Deutsch, Brad and Alan Antin and many others. It's also where I had the opportunity to meet a gentleman named Carl Galletti for the first time.

That chance meeting led to a joint venture with Carl two or three years later where I took over his hard-to-find marketing books catalog. Fast forward to 1999, and Carl decided to put on his first Internet Marketing Superconference at the old Las Vegas Hilton hotel and asked me if I would come out and set up a marketing bookstore at his event and handle the back-of-the-room sales. I had only a vague idea of what that entailed, but I hadn't been to Vegas before and it sounded like a great opportunity to learn and meet some new folks. So I agreed to come out and help Carl.

That one event evolved into the eventual formation of Speaker Fulfillment Services (now Get.Ship.Done.) as we know it today. And it's still evolving. Some of the speakers at Carl's event, who were event promoters in their own right, saw what we were doing and asked us if we could help at their event.

As a result, I had the opportunity to handle the back-of-the-room sales tables at nearly 150 events over the next fifteen to twenty years. I got to personally know many of the biggest names in internet and information marketing. People like Alex Mandossian, Armand Morin, Frank Kern, Ryan Deiss, Mike Filsaime, Joel Comm, John Assaraf, Jim Edwards, Suzanne Evans, Elizabeth McCormick and many more.

They knew I was doing order fulfillment for my own online ventures (I developed the first portal website in the plant engineering and maintenance industry way back in 1995) and so they encouraged me to form the fulfillment company and provide those services to them. The rest, as they say, is history.

You can find out more information about Get.Ship. Done. and its associated brands online at GetShipDone. com

For more information about Bret and his available services please visit BretRidgway.com and be sure to follow him on social media.

www.linkedin.com/in/bretridgway
www.facebook.com/bretridgway
twitter.com/bridgway
instagram.com/bretridgway

Also Authored or Coauthored by Bret Ridgway

View from the Back: 101 Tips for Event Promoters Who Want to Dramatically Increase Back-of-the-Room Sales

50 Biggest Mistakes I See Information Marketers Make

50 Biggest Website Mistakes Online Business Owners Make

Mistakes Authors Make

ABCs of Speaking

Here's How I Did It! Volume 2

Consuming Your Content

From Novice Speaker to Stage Ready Pro Masterclass

Are you a successful business owner who wants to launch a speaking career or add speaking to the marketing mix of your business? Or simply someone with a powerful message you want to share and you just aren't sure how the speaking industry really works?

As a twenty-five-year veteran of the speaking industry, I've seen it all. I've been an attendee at hundreds of events and I've managed the back sales table at around 150 internet and information marketing conferences. I've also handled product fulfillment for many of the biggest names in the industry, so I've seen first-hand what they do well and what they don't do so well.

If you're ready to take the shortcut to speaking success and want to find out how the industry really works and learn what you need to do to be gig ready, then it's time to sign up for the "Getting Gig Ready for the Novice Speaker" masterclass.

This six-week course is just $1997, and each session will run approximately one hour. Here's a breakdown of what you'll learn week by week:

Week 1—Overview of the Speaking Industry

- Fee vs. Free Speakers
- Virtual vs. In Person Events
- Podcasting
- Demographics & Key Metrics
- Dealing with Event Promoters
- Defining Your Signature Speech
- Your Goal as a Speakers

Week 2—Pieces You Need to Put into Place

- Website
- List Building Bribe
- Social Media
- Media Kit/Press Room
- Contact Channels
- Stories
- Book
- Branding

Week 3—Getting Gigs

- Speaker Bureaus
- Relationships
- List Building
- Vas
- Nurturing Your Flock

- Resources for Getting Gigs

Week 4—Backend Products/Services
- Consulting
- Coaching
- Masterminds
- Membership Sites
- Training Courses
- Masterclasses
- Home Study Courses
- Product Consumption
- Selling Products in Development

Week 5—Mistakes to Avoid
- Back Pocket Speech
- The $375,000 Mistake
- The $300,000 Mistake
- Prima Donnas
- Killing a List
- Repurposing Your Assets
- Outsourcing
- Who's Handling the Money?

Week 6—Virtual Events
- Lighting
- Interaction
- Tools

Week 7—Having a Book
- Consumability
- Lead Generation (Name capture mechanisms)
- Importance of Your Cover
- Getting Amazon Reviews
- Monetizing Your Book

Week 8—Wrap Up and Q & A
- Quick Review of First 7 Weeks
- Prioritizing Your Next Steps
- Resources Available to Help You

The dates for the next session of the Masterclass are still being determined, so simply scan the QR code on the next page and you'll be taken to a page where you can add yourself to the notification list for the next session.

**Scan QR Code to Get on
The Notification List for the Next
"From Novice Speaker to Stage Ready Pro"
Masterclass**

or

**Visit BretRidgway.com and
click on the Consulting Tab**

A free ebook edition
is available with the
purchase of this book.

Print & Digital Together Forever.

Snap a photo   Free ebook   Read anywhere

Printed in the USA
CPSIA information can be obtained
at www.ICGtesting.com
JSHW021518021023
49513JS00005B/346